Notorious Assassins: The Life

By Charles River Editors

THE ASSASSINATION OF PRESIDENT LINCOLN.
AT FORD'S THEATRE WASHINGTON D.C. APRIL 14TH 1865.

About Charles River Editors

Charles River Editors was founded by Harvard and MIT alumni to provide superior editing and original writing services, with the expertise to create digital content for publishers across a vast range of subject matter. In addition to providing original digital content for third party publishers, Charles River Editors republishes civilization's greatest literary works, bringing them to a new generation via ebooks.

Introduction

John Wilkes Booth (1838-1865)

"Right or wrong. God judge me, not man. For be my motive good or bad, of one thing I am sure, the lasting condemnation of the North." – John Wilkes Booth

Before the night of April 14, 1865, John Wilkes Booth was one of the most famous actors of his time, and President Abraham Lincoln had even watched him perform, but his most significant performance at a theater did not take place on the stage. That night, Booth became one of history's most infamous assassins when he shot President Lincoln at Ford's Theatre in Washington, D.C.

Booth was a member of the prominent 19th century Booth theatrical family from Maryland, and he was a well-known actor throughout much of the country by the 1860s. But Booth was also a Confederate sympathizer who dabbled in espionage, and he was increasingly outraged at the Lincoln Administration. Although Robert E. Lee had surrendered the Army of Northern Virginia at Appomattox a few days earlier, an action often cited as the end of the Civil War, Booth believed the war was not yet over because Confederate soldiers under General Joseph E. Johnston were still fighting, and the flamboyant actor hoped his conspiracy could strike the kind of blow that might turn the Confederacy's fate around. Early plans to kidnap and ransom President Lincoln ultimately gave way to a wide ranging conspiracy by Booth and a small group to kill Lincoln and other top officials in a bid to decapitate the federal government and help the South.

Perhaps not surprisingly, the actor's flair for the dramatic came at a cost to the plot. It took almost no time for the shocked public and the federal government to begin unraveling Booth's conspiracy, which had mostly faltered from the beginning. Following the shooting, America's most famous manhunt commenced, a 12 day pursuit that became the stuff of legends and controversy itself. Eight others were eventually tried for their alleged involvement in the plot and convicted, and four were hanged shortly thereafter as a result of some of the nation's most famous trials.

Booth's crime has ensured his notoriety, but it has also overshadowed his life and career, not to mention his Civil War activities and the evolution of his plot. *Notorious Assassins: The Life of John Wilkes Booth* comprehensively covers his life and career, as well as the origins of the plot, the assassination of Lincoln, and the manhunt and trials that followed. Along with pictures of the important people and places, you will learn about the Lincoln's assassin like you never have before, in no time at all.

Chapter 1: Early Years

No matter the century, it seems that being the child of a celebrity has its own set of challenges, and such was the case for John Wilkes Booth, the ninth of ten children born to Mary Ann and Junius Brutus Booth. Furthermore, John Wilkes was named after a distant relative known in Britain as a radical writer and politician.

John Wilkes

When his son was born, Junius, whose middle name instantly brings to mind one of Julius Caesar's assassins, was one of the world's most famous actors. A native of England, he had moved to the United States under rather complicated circumstances in 1821; having been swept off his feet by Mary Ann Holmes, he left his wife and child behind and started a new life in Maryland.

Junius Brutus Booth in 1850

For Junius, escaping his past would not be so easy, as his entire family would discover over a decade later, but he was as successful of an actor in the United States as he was in England. When John Wilkes was born on May 10, 1838, Junius was doing well enough to afford a home in rural Maryland, as well as a house in the city of Baltimore. John Wilkes was born on what the Booths called "The Farm," a four-room log cabin located on 150 acres of land in Harford County, Maryland, northeast of Baltimore. Long before there was air conditioning, theaters typically closed in the summer, and it was in the off-season that Junius and his family would head for The Farm. When he returned to the stage at the end of the summer, Mary Ann and the children moved back into their house in Baltimore.

By all accounts, John Wilkes was the favorite out of all of the Booth children, and much of his early childhood was spent in the company of his mother, who lavished the boy with affection. His father was one of the hardest working entertainers in the country and rarely turned down a job, no matter how small the part or how remote the location of the theater, which helped his fame spread to even the smallest frontier towns. Although Junius was frequently gone, he clearly had a big influence on his children. As the country would quickly discover, despite Junius's own wishes, three of his sons, including John Wilkes, followed in his footsteps and began their own noteworthy careers on the stage.

It is estimated that Junius gave nearly 2,800 performances in his life, which seems inconceivable in an era without modern travel. Acting was an exhausting career, which was true for him as well as his sons, and it involved touring at a time when travel was far from luxurious. Theaters were either hot or drafty, and getting paid could occasionally be difficult. Perhaps that is why Junius loved The Farm so much. He seemed the happiest tending the animals and the gardens, which John Wilkes and his siblings were also expected to do when they were old enough to help. It was far from the typical 19th century farm, however, because Junius refused to kill anything. He could not bear to kill an animal for food and thus lived his life as a vegetarian. He told his children that even flies must have their purpose and tried to convince them that insects should not be killed.

The fact that Junius literally would not hurt a fly was just one of the reasons that he was considered an eccentric. He also had a tendency to descend into bouts of bizarre behavior, sometimes while on stage. Most of the time, Junius was a captivating actor with the rare ability to convince an audience that he was, indeed, the character he was playing. However, he was also known to suddenly step out of character and address the audience as himself. Other times, he would disappear, only to be found wandering in the woods while in costume. Junius was known to have a fondness for alcohol, which may have been at least part of the reason for this behavior.

Given his father's profession and the various roles he played, it was only natural that young John Wilkes had an active imagination. He liked to make up stories and speeches, and he was known to charge at bushes and trees, sometimes carrying a sword that a soldier had brought back from the Mexican-American War, all while delivering a rousing speech to anyone within earshot. Given the chance, the active young boy would have likely chosen to stay in the city instead of retreating to The Farm, because Baltimore buzzed with activity in the 1840s. Already benefitting from a strong oyster canning industry, the marketing of a popular "family flour" in 1844 led to Baltimore becoming a center of international trade. John Wilkes thrived in the close-knit neighborhood on Exeter Street, and nearly everyone who encountered him found him to be a pleasant and engaging child.

Slavery was still the law of the land in the 1840s but the debate over its potential end was well underway, and John Wilkes grew up hearing both sides of the argument. After the Mexican-American War ended in 1848, the sectional crisis was brewing like never before, with California and the newly-acquired Mexican territory now ready to be organized into states. The country was once again left trying to figure out how to do it without offsetting the slave-free state balance. With the new territory acquired in the Mexican-American War, pro and anti-slavery groups were at an impasse. The Whig Party, including freshman Congressman Abraham Lincoln, supported the Wilmot Proviso, which would have banned slavery in all territory acquired from Mexico, but the slave states would have none of it. Even after Texas was annexed as a slave state, the enormous new territory would doubtless contain many other new states, and the North hoped to limit slavery as much as possible in the new territories.

Lincoln

As it turned out, the issue would be resolved temporarily by the Compromise of 1850, which was authored by "The Great Compromiser", Henry Clay. In addition to admitting California to the Union as a free state to balance with Texas, it allowed Utah and New Mexico to decide the issue of slavery on the basis of what became known as "popular sovereignty", which meant the settlers could vote on whether their state should be a free state or slave state. The Compromise also abolished the slave trade (though not the existence of slavery itself) in Washington, D.C.

Members of Congress agreed with select measures of the bill, and a majority of different coalitions existed for each idea. Northerners supported abolishing the slave trade and reducing Texas' borders, while Southerners liked a strengthened Fugitive Slave Act and popular sovereignty. Together, though, the bill could not be passed as a single Compromise. Senator Stephen Douglas thus took the helm and introduced each bill as a separate act, allowing the totality of the Compromise of 1850 to pass later in the year. A spirit of Compromise prevailed, and the country felt that it had brokered a lasting peace that had decided the issue of slavery in a way that was agreeable to both sides.

At the time, Maryland was both a slave state and a border state, and its residents were a volatile mix of northern industrialism and southern agrarianism who were deeply divided on slavery's future. Talk of secession among the southern states had already begun but there were too many Northerners to swing Maryland firmly into the secessionist corner. Still, there were more than enough Southerners to make Maryland a hostile environment for anyone who voiced abolitionist sentiments or the possibility of slavery coming to an end.

For his own part, Junius did not own slaves, but he did lease their services from slave owners. Junius also showed a level of respect to African-Americans that was practically unheard of in his era. He built comfortable servants quarters on The Farm and did not hesitate to share a meal with a man or woman of another race. When a young slave girl was on her deathbed and asked to see Junius's daughter Asia one last time, Junius took Asia to the girl. Years later, those that worked for Junius remembered him as a kind man and a fair employer, but many whites of the era thought that Junius was simply going mad. When John Wilkes later became the head of the Booth family, he did not show the same deference to servants and slaves as his father.

Asia

The area where John Wilkes did align with his father was in the desire to perform. He and his brother Edwin staged performances for their Baltimore neighborhood, and by using costumes, props, and even animals that most of the parents did not realize they were contributing to the cause, John Wilkes, Edwin, and other neighborhood boys created a "traveling" acting troupe. They charged one cent for admission for children, who made up the majority of their audience, and two cents for the parents, with their performances being held in the local horse stables, cellars, and backyards.

Edwin Booth portraying Iago in *Othello*

John Wilkes was also given the opportunity to perform at school. His early school days were spent at the nearby Bel Air Academy with his brother Joseph, but in 1849, 11 year-old John Wilkes was enrolled at the Milton Academy in Sparks, just north of Baltimore. Milton was a Quaker college prep boarding school with a focus on the classics, where students were required to read and recite from the Ancient Greeks such as Herodotus, Cicero, and Livy. His first public performance was at a school picnic at Milton; with his mother and sister Asia in attendance, John Wilkes gave a well-received dramatic reading as Shylock in Shakespeare's *The Merchant of Venice*.

John Wilkes was a bright student, but he was a bit indifferent about studying at times. At Bel Air, the headmaster described the teen as "[n]ot deficient in intelligence, but disinclined to take advantage of the educational opportunities offered him". With that said, like many students, it depended on the topic. When it came to something he was interested in, John Wilkes was always up for a challenge, and one of those challenges was memorizing all 1,300 lines of Lord Byron's *The Giaour.* It was an interesting choice of poems for John Wilkes to memorize, because much of 19th century society considered Lord Byron's romantic themes scandalous, but Mary Ann told her children that it was his poetry that convinced her to marry their father.

However, the Booth children were about to find out that their parents' marriage was far from conventional.

Chapter 2: The Return of Adelaide Booth

In 1846, when John Wilkes was 8 years old, he and his siblings learned the truth about their parents' relationship, which was brought about by the arrival of Marie Christine Adelaide Delannoy. Adelaide, as she was known, left Liverpool, England on the steamship *Great Western*, and after arriving in New York, she continued on to Baltimore to see her son, Richard. To all who asked, Adelaide introduced herself as Mrs. Junius Booth.

Junius and Adelaide had been married in England in 1815 and had two children together, though Richard was the only one that survived. Six years later, Junius met Mary Ann as she sold flowers outside of the theater where he performed, and they quickly fell in love and made plans to run away to America. Junius said nothing of Mary Ann to Adelaide. He had said only that British audiences were growing tired of him and that he wanted to see how he could do in front of American audiences. Junius had promised his wife he would send money every month, which he did faithfully for 20 years.

However, when the money stopped coming, Adelaide did a little detective work. She subscribed to American newspapers, assuming that if her husband was making a living as an actor, his name would appear in the paper. Sure enough, Adelaide discovered that Junius was still alive and well and earning a good living as an actor. She sent Richard to America to monitor both his father and his father's money.

Richard did find Junius, but somehow he spent three years traveling with his father on the road without discovering the existence of Mary Ann, John Wilkes, and his siblings. It was only after someone accused Richard of being Junius's illegitimate son that he discovered the truth: Junius had a family in Baltimore. Richard contacted his mother immediately and broke the news.

When she arrived in America, Adelaide seemed to be far more interested in compensation for her troubles than in reuniting with Junius. She threatened a lawsuit but said she would not sue if Junius gave her a lump sum payment upfront, as well as continuing to pay a monthly stipend. The Booths felt they had no choice but to do this, and the only way that they could make sure that Junius did not spend all of the money he made while on the road was to have someone constantly watch over him. Junius, Jr., or "June" as he was called, had been the one to watch over his father, but he was getting started with his own acting career. That left 12 year-old Edwin and 8 year-old John Wilkes. However, Mary Ann was so devoted to John Wilkes that she would not entertain the option of sending him on the road for months at a time, so Edwin was chosen to accompany his father and John Wilkes stayed in Baltimore.

By this time, news of Junius's double life had spread, leaving John Wilkes to bear much of the brunt of the taunts and accusations that he was a bastard. Some even questioned whether or not he had the legitimate right to the Booth family name, and the fact that Adelaide and Richard remained in Baltimore only served to keep the gossip mill churning. Finally, in 1851, Adelaide granted Junius a divorce, and on John Wilkes' 13th birthday, Junius and Mary Ann were legally married.

The incident left its mark on John Wilkes, who was proud of his father and proud of his name. Having his legacy and the honor of his family challenged was hurtful, and it left him determined to reclaim the respectability of the Booth name. As if making a statement for all to see that he was a Booth and proud of it, John Wilkes used India Ink to permanently tattoo his initials on the back of his left hand.

Chapter 3: The Death of Junius Booth

In 1852, John Wilkes was 14 years old and had completed his education at Milton Academy. Junius and Mary Ann were intent on him continuing his education, so John Wilkes was enrolled in St. Timothy's Hall. The Catonsville, Maryland boarding school sent a lengthy booklet to the parents of each applicant that explained the school rules. Much was expected of the boys at St. Timothy's, and parents were asked to respect the fact that while the children were at school, it was the headmaster and faculty, not the parents, who were in charge. The school's prospectus said that St. Timothy's required good morals and strict discipline from its students. That discipline included wearing military-style uniforms and referring to the incoming students as cadets.

Booth adapted well to the regimented environment of military school, which ultimately left him with a desire for order and an appreciation for chain-of-command. He got along well with his classmates, including Samuel Arnold, and Booth would later recruit Arnold to take part in his failed conspiracy to kidnap President Abraham Lincoln. Ultimately, however, Booth spent only one year there because not long after he was enrolled, his father died on board a steamship to Cincinnati. It is believed that Junius drank polluted water while on the trip, and with no doctor available, there was little that could be done for him.

Samuel Arnold

Mary Ann blamed Edwin and June for abandoning their father, and by this point, both sons were in California focusing on their own careers. Mary Ann told them not to come home, and they did not return for several years, leaving John Wilkes feeling responsible for being the man of the family. After his year at St. Timothy's, he returned to the family's new home, called Tudor Hall, in Bel Air. Despite the fact this was a difficult time for the Booths, and it was only made more challenging by a lawsuit brought by a local architect over a dispute regarding payment for work on the new family home, John Wilkes was surprisingly cheerful. He spent much of his free time riding his horse and reading the poetry texts that he brought with him from St. Timothy's. In his letters to friends, he wrote of girls that he had his eye on, the fun he was having hunting and drinking, and how he was keeping watch over his family.

Tudor Hall

However, Booth showed that he was not like his father when it came to showing respect to the African-American laborers that worked on the family property. He was a firm believer in the power of rank and the authority that one man held over another. While he rarely said anything, his body language and the fact that he could barely manage to stay in the same room when it was time to eat said it all. He was not about to share a meal with servants. Unlike when Junius was the family patriarch, the Booth family was a very unpopular employer with John Wilkes in charge.

Booth also began to show some political leanings at this point in his life. Certainly, political turmoil was all around him, and even an adolescent would have been hard-pressed to ignore the major issues of the day. One of those issues was immigration and the rise of nativism. In the mid-1850s, as Irish immigrants fled the starvation and massive unemployment caused by the Great Potato Famine, many Americans expressed concern that the U.S. was attracting more immigrants than it could handle. Secret societies of nativists led to a political group called the Know-Nothings, a name supposedly stemming from the agreement among the secret society members who vowed to "know nothing" if asked about their activities. John Wilkes and Asia both attended Know-Nothing meetings in Baltimore, but their involvement did not progress beyond that.

Chapter 4: Acting Career

For John Wilkes, politics took a backseat to his budding acting career. Motivated by letters from Edwin and June, who were having their own successes acting on the West Coast, he joined the Charles Street Theatre in Baltimore, and at 17, he made his debut as the Earl of Richmond in Shakespeare's *Richard III* on August 14, 1855. Still, John Wilkes only appeared in one scene (during which he forgot some of his lines), and the Charles Street Theatre was hardly Baltimore's finest, leading his mother to think he was not truly ready for the stage. She accused the acting troupe manager of trying to capitalize on the Booth name for his own gain, an idea not lost on the young man either. He also recognized that in the early stages of his career, there was no way that he would be able to measure up to his father's legend, so he went by the stage name of J.B. Wilkes while he was still learning the ropes

In 1857, John Wilkes put the family home in Bel Air up for sale, with the advertisement prominently noting that the house once belonged to the late "J.B. Booth", even though Junius died before it was completed. Regardless, he was taking his acting career to Philadelphia, and his mother and sisters were going with him. Booth joined the Wheatley Arch Street Theatre as a stock theatre actor for a salary of $80 a week, which was not much for supporting a family but a respectable sum for a new actor. It would not be long before he was making far more than that, because he was quickly on his way to becoming one of the brightest stars in the country.

Historians differ on whether or not Booth's year in Philadelphia was a success. Some say that it was a disastrous experience for him, but if that was true, it would have been difficult for him to continue on the stage. What is known is that fellow actors and the paying patrons had few complaints about his performances, and it's likely his reputation as a well-liked actor was an asset to the company. Booth also had a sense of humor, turning around a bad case of stage fright in his first performance at the Arch Street Theatre while delivering his first lines in *Lucrezia Borgia*, "Madame, I am Pondolfio Pet—Pedolfio Pat—Pantuchio Ped—dammit! Who am I?" The botched lines sent the audience into hysterics.

Booth performed dozens of times during his first year, and many of the roles he played in 1858 had a political theme. His characters would often be in the fight against tyranny and oppression. Some, like *Hamlet* and *Julius Caesar*, dealt with the assassination of political leaders, and Booth relished playing Brutus. Fighting a perceived political oppressor was a theme that Booth would come to incorporate into his personal life.

The Booth brothers acting in Shakespeare's *Caesar*. John Wilkes is on the far left.

Booth joined the Marshall Theatre in Richmond, Virginia in 1858, which had a better reputation than the Arch Street Theatre. Like the Arch Street Theatre, the Marshall Theatre was a stock company, which required Booth to learn 18 parts in the two weeks leading up to the beginning of the season. However, Booth was almost certainly happy to have the opportunity to work for a company with better marketing and better talent than he had in Philadelphia. He was also among people he knew, since all of the company's managers were from Baltimore, as were many of the back-of-the-house staff. By all accounts, Booth learned quickly, performed well, and was a star on the rise. Historian Jim Bishop noted that Booth "developed into an outrageous scene stealer, but he played his parts with such heightened enthusiasm that the audiences idolized him", and he even played the part of Horatio alongside his brother Edwin in *Hamlet* at the Marshall Theatre.

Critics were mixed on Booth's natural abilities, but whatever deficiencies he had were obscured by his magnetism and charisma. Recognized as one of the most handsome men in the country, Booth self-confidently used his physicality to great effect, engaging in swordplay during some scenes that actually left him bloodied.

Meanwhile, as Booth's fame and fortunes grew, political tension surrounding slavery continued to rise as well. By 1853 and 1854, the Compromise of 1850 had come under withering assault. The Compromise had not settled all territory needed to be admitted for statehood, and at the time the Compromise was signed, little was known about the quality of the new territory. By 1854, however, it was apparent that Arizona and New Mexico would be of little use for agriculture, and thus of little use for slaves. On the other hand, while the states slated for slavery could not use them, advocates of slavery pointed out that Kansas and Nebraska, which had been designated to enter the Union as Free States, were extremely well-suited to slave-based agriculture. The South thus decided to use the issue of expanding railroads as a bargaining chip in adjusting the fate of slavery in Kansas and Nebraska.

In an attempt to find compromise and organize the center of North America – Kansas and Nebraska – without offsetting the slave-free balance, Senator Stephen Douglas proposed the Kansas-Nebraska Act. The Kansas-Nebraska Act eliminated the Missouri Compromise line of 1820, which had stipulated for over a generation that states north of the line would be free and states south of it *could* have slavery. This was essential to maintaining the balance of slave and free states in the Union, but the Kansas-Nebraska Act, ignored the line completely and proposed that all new territories be organized by popular sovereignty. Settlers could vote whether they wanted their state to be slave or free.

When popular sovereignty became the standard in Kansas and Nebraska, the primary result was that thousands of zealous pro-slavery and anti-slavery advocates both moved to Kansas to influence the vote, creating a dangerous and ultimately deadly mix. Numerous attacks took place between the two sides, and many pro-slavery Missourians organized attacks on Kansas towns just across the border. The most famous and infamous of them all was John Brown, perhaps the most controversial American of the 19th century. A radical abolitionist, Brown organized a small band of like-minded followers and fought with the armed groups of pro-slavery men in Kansas for several months, including a notorious incident known as the Pottawatomie Massacre, in which Brown's supporters murdered five men. Over 50 people died before John Brown left the territory, which ultimately entered the Union as a free state in 1859.

John Brown

While Brown acted militantly, politicians across the North, primarily Whigs and Free Soilers, were aghast over the Kansas-Nebraska Act. The suggestion that Congress could extend slavery into any unsettled territory violated some of their dearest held principles that slavery should not extend further. Whigs and Free Soilers in the North quickly coalesced against the "Slave Power", believing Southern influence in Washington had gone too far and now held the government in a strangle-hold. This coalescence first became known as the "anti-Nebraska" group, but it quickly vowed to form a new political party dedicated to keeping the Western territories free from slavery. They called themselves the Republicans.

After plotting to arm the slaves of Virginia and lead a slave revolt, in July 1859, Brown traveled to Harper's Ferry under an assumed name and waited for recruits, but he struggled to get even 20 people to join him. Rather than call off the plan, however, Brown went ahead with it. That fall, Brown and his men used hundreds of rifles to seize the armory at Harper's Ferry, but the plan went haywire from the start, and word of his attack quickly spread. Local pro-slavery men formed a militia and pinned Brown and his men down while they were still at the armory. After being called to Harpers Ferry, Robert E. Lee took decisive command of a troop of marines stationed there, surrounded the arsenal, and gave Brown the opportunity to surrender peaceably. When Brown refused, Lee ordered the doors be broken down and Brown taken captive, an affair that reportedly lasted just three minutes. A few of Brown's men were killed, but Brown was taken alive.

The fallout from John Brown's raid on Harpers Ferry was intense. Southerners had long suspected that abolitionists hoped to arm the slaves and use violence to abolish slavery, and Brown's raid seemed to confirm that. Meanwhile, much of the northern press praised Brown for his actions. In the South, conspiracy theories ran wild about who had supported the raid, and many believed prominent abolitionist Republicans had been behind the raid as well. On the day of his execution, Brown wrote, "I, John Brown, am now quite certain that the crimes of this guilty land will never be purged away but with blood. I had, as I now think vainly, flattered myself that without very much bloodshed it might be done."

Two weeks before Brown was due to be executed, word spread that a group of abolitionists intended to march into Charlestown and set Brown free. The call for the militia went out again, and volunteer troops began to flood into Charlestown. Booth had a front row seat as the Richmond Grays prepared to deploy, because the railroad tracks ran right past the Marshall Theatre. He had a clear view of the men climbing into the cars and watched for a while as the area in front of the theater was alive with activity. It would be a stretch to say that Booth was politically active up to this point in his life, but there is no doubt that he considered himself to be a man of the South. Through the time he spent touring the South, he was immersed in their way of thinking and sympathetic to their cause.

It was at this point that something in Booth began to stir. Without a word to the manager of the theater troupe, he went to the train and tried to get on board, but he was told that it was reserved for militia only. When Booth said he was willing to buy a uniform, a jacket and pants were scrounged up for him and Booth joined the militia that was bound for Charlestown. A local reporter recognized Booth and said in the Richmond *Enquirer* that he, "threw down the sock and buskin, and shouldered his musket with the Grays to the scene of the deadly conflict."

It turned out that there was no deadly conflict. The Grays simply proved security at the courthouse where Brown was being detained because Charlestown was overrun with militia at this point. Hundreds of men kept a watch for anyone who might try to interfere with Brown's execution. When it came time to hang Brown, Booth was there. In fact, he stood just a few yards away from Thomas Jonathan Jackson, who was in command of the troops present at Brown's hanging after being ordered to Charlestown in November. After Brown's hanging, the man who would later earn undying fame in the Civil War as Stonewall Jackson began to believe war was inevitable, but he wrote his aunt, "I think we have great reason for alarm, but my trust is in God; and I cannot think that He will permit the madness of men to interfere so materially with the Christian labors of this country at home and abroad."

Booth watched the trap door open, and though Brown was hanged, he died slowly, with blood spilling from his mouth, Booth later admitted to feeling a bit faint, but he was also impressed with Brown. Even if he did not agree with what he had done, Booth admired Brown's bravery at the moment of his death.

Of course, Booth would also later exaggerate the role he played in John Brown's raid and execution. As the Confederacy's chances were quickly dwindling near the end of 1864 and the beginning of 1865, Booth wrote in a letter:

"When I aided in the capture and execution of JOHN BROWN (who was a murderer on our Western border, and who was fairly tried and convicted, before an impartial judge and jury, of treason, and who, by the way, has since been made a god), I was proud of my little share in the transaction, for I deemed it my duty, and that I was helping our common country to perform an act of justice. But what was a crime in poor JOHN BROWN is now considered (by themselves) as the greatest and only virtue of the whole Republican Party. Strange transmigration! Vice to become a virtue, simply because more indulge in it

I thought men, as now, that the Abolitionists were the only traitors in the land, and that the entire party deserved the same fate of poor old BROWN, not because they wish to abolish slavery but on account of the means they have ever endeavored to use to effect that abolition. If BROWN were living I doubt whether he himself would set slavery against the Union. Most or many in the North do, and openly curse the Union, if the South are to return and retain a single right guarantied to them by every tie which we once revered as sacred. The South can make no choice. It is either extermination or slavery for themselves (worse than death) to draw from. I know my choice."

As the consequence of abruptly walking out on his job at the Marshall Theatre, Booth was fired, and when some members of the Richmond Grays met with the manager and asked for Booth to be reinstated, there may have been a moment's hesitation for Booth. He was not sure that he wanted to act anymore and thought the military might be the right path for him, but he did ultimately take his old job back.

By the summer of 1860, as Abraham Lincoln was making his bid for the presidency, Booth's career took another step forward when he was given the job of the leading man of Matthew W. Canning's touring company. The company toured the South, which gave Booth even more opportunity to absorb the arguments, the debates, and the viewpoints of the Southerners, as well as make more contacts with people. The South had made its feelings about Lincoln very clear. He had never claimed to be an abolitionist and held too much regard for the Constitution to simply outlaw slavery, but his remark that the country could not survive "half slave and half free," was enough of a threat to the slaveholding states. By the Fall of 1860, everyone could see potential secession on the horizon.

Meanwhile, Booth made a successful debut for Canning's troupe as the lead in *Romeo and Juliet*, but his acting career nearly came to an end in October 1860, when Canning, Booth, and an actor named Johnny Albaugh were in their hotel in Columbus, Georgia, preparing for a performance of *Hamlet*. As Canning took a nap on the bed, Booth saw his gun sticking out of his pocket. Wanting to show his acting colleagues what a great shot he was, Booth took Canning's gun, aimed at a mark on the wall, and squeezed the trigger.

The noise shook Canning out of his sleep, and he sat up to see Booth holding his gun. Canning told Booth to give it back to him, but Booth refused. Instead, Booth convinced Canning to hold the gun while he tried to scrape some rust off of the barrel with his pocket knife. At that point, the gun accidentally went off, sending a bullet into Booth's thigh and just narrowly missing his femoral artery. Even still, Booth was badly injured, so Johnny Albaugh played *Hamlet* that night and took Booth's place as the leading man while Booth spent nearly all of the acting season recuperating in his hotel room. It was not until the end of the season that Booth returned to the stage, limping out to stage in

Columbus to recite a monologue from *Julius Caesar*.

By the time Booth joined the company in Montgomery, Alabama, he had recovered enough to perform to rave reviews. He was the Canning company's star attraction, earning the praise of critics for his performances and the admiration of more than one Southern belle for his dark, handsome looks. He was in Montgomery when the election results came in and Abraham Lincoln won the presidency, despite not even appearing on the ballot in some of the southern states. It is likely that Booth read the headline of the local paper and heard the cries from the local citizens calling for Alabama to secede.

Booth wrote his own feelings on the issue in a speech, although the speech was never delivered in public. Perhaps that was not his intent. However, Booth shared the same feelings of many in the South, and even some people in the North. According to Booth, abolitionists were to blame for the country's division. Had the abolitionists not written articles calling for slavery's end, refused to abide by the Fugitive Slave Law that required their assistance in returning runaway slaves, and aided in the escape of slaves in outright defiance of the law, all would be well. By stirring the pot with talk about ending slavery, they had created a division that would likely take a war to repair.

Despite his father's opposition to slavery, which Edwin shared, Booth took the paternal approach that many slaveholders used to justify holding African-Americans in bondage. Booth believed Africans were better off in the United States than in Africa, and that white slave owners were like their fathers, who knew what was best for them. According to Booth and those that shared this view, abolitionists were not only harming the country, they were harming the slaves themselves by potentially removing them from the system that provided for their most basic needs.

With the election of Republican candidate Abraham Lincoln as president on November 6, 1860, many Southerners considered it the final straw. Someone they knew as a "Black Republican", leader of a party whose central platform was to stop the spread of slavery to new states, was now set to be inaugurated as President in March. Throughout the fall and winter of 1860, Southern calls for secession became increasingly serious. In a last-ditched effort to save the Union, Kentucky's Senator John Crittenden tried to assume the stateliness of his predecessor Henry Clay. Crittenden, however, proved to be no Henry Clay: his proposal that a Constitutional Amendment reinstate the Missouri Compromise line and extend it to the Pacific failed. President Buchanan supported the measure, but President-Elect Lincoln said he refused to allow the further expansion of slavery under any conditions.

The Crittenden Compromise failed on December 18. Two days later, South Carolina seceded from the Union. President Buchanan sat on his hands, believing the Southern states had no right to secede, but that the Federal government had no effective power to prevent secession. In January, Mississippi, Florida, Alabama, Georgia, Louisiana and Kansas followed South Carolina's lead. The Confederacy was formed on February 4th, in Montgomery, Alabama, with former Secretary of War Jefferson Davis as its President. On February 23rd, Texas joined the Confederacy.

As the Southern states began to secede, Booth continued to tour and perform, and at one point, while he was in Albany, New York, he found himself in the same city as the president-elect. Lincoln was there to have dinner with governor while Booth was playing the role of Pescara in *The Apostate*.

Lincoln left Albany without incident, even as a group of Southerners was plotting an assassination attempt that would have taken place in Baltimore had it not been thwarted by detective Allan Pinkerton. However, Booth was far removed from that plot, and the only person he hurt in Albany was himself. After having finally recovered from his gunshot wound, Booth fell onto a sword during a scene in the play and carved out three inches of muscle near his armpit. Despite the wound, Booth returned to the stage that next night with his injured arm tied to his side.

Chapter 5: An Acting Career Ends

Booth in the 1860s

In November 1863, the Union's fortunes seemed to be on the rise. The victories at Gettysburg and Vicksburg months earlier in July were decisive turning points that would lead to the South's demise. That month, Lincoln would travel to Gettysburg to deliver his immortal Gettysburg Address, but he also attended a play, *The Marble Heart*, from his presidential box at the newly opened Ford's Theatre in Washington D.C. The lead role was played by one of the country's most famous actors, John Wilkes Booth.

The presidential box at Ford's Theatre

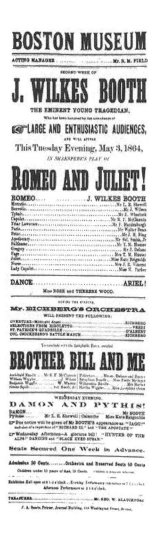

A May 1863 poster advertising Booth's role in *Romeo and Juliet*

It is difficult to pinpoint any one speech or event that led Booth to focus all of his rage about the crumbling of the South on Lincoln. Some say that by the time he performed at Ford's Theater in Washington, D.C. before the president, he was angry enough to turn and point his finger at Lincoln during a line he seemed to intend especially for the president's ears, but this story sounds conveniently apocryphal given the knowledge of his involvement in the Lincoln assassination. What is clear is that Booth was not shy about voicing his Confederate sympathies and his venom toward the North throughout the Civil War. On one tour in St. Louis, Booth was actually detained for "treasonous" remarks after he had vocally expressed his desire for Lincoln and the government to go to hell. His partisanship during the war became so bitter that older brother Edwin, who stayed loyal to the Union and wouldn't perform in the South, often avoided confrontation with him. There have also been those who argued Booth was crazy or fanatical, but that is also a difficult view to support because his views were no different than those held by millions of other Americans. The difference for Booth was that he was apparently not able to contain his rage, and he had an inflated sense of his own self-worth outside of the acting world.

Booth was a dashing actor, well-versed in Shakespeare, and a man so handsome that he constantly received fan mail from women he made swoon, but he had accomplished nothing outside the world of acting. Nevertheless, Booth's interest in acting began to wane in 1864. When his agent wrote to him and asked him what had become of his desire and passion for the stage, Booth questioned acting's worth not just for himself but the point of it all for everyone in general. Certainly, had Booth wanted to continue his acting career, he could have done so. He was making enough money to invest in oil wells, although he ended up losing more than he made, and at one point he earned $20,000 a year, the modern day equivalent of almost half a million dollars. Booth was also famous enough that women waited for him to come out of the theater after his performances, sometimes worked up to the point of tearing pieces of his clothes away. All of this runs counter to the argument that Booth became political because he was frustrated over the direction of his acting career.

Booth had promised his mother that he would not fight in the war, and he kept that promise, but he felt that he had to do something, so he started doing work for the Confederate Underground. It was easy for Booth to be a courier for this loosely organized network of Confederates because he was always on the move, so he was able to use his fame and position as an actor to help smuggle goods into the South past the ongoing Union blockade. Still, there were plenty of Southerners who had the same resentment of the North and engaged in Confederate activities on a much higher level, and despite Booth's ardent pro-Southern views, he continued to be welcomed and lauded in the North. Of course, these small-scale activities left Booth fancying himself a Confederate spy during the early years of the war.

It was not until the Election of 1864 that Booth began plotting a daring move. After Vicksburg and Gettysburg had left the Confederacy's hopes of an outright victory in the war looking highly unlikely, the South held out hope that Lincoln would lose his reelection and be replaced by a Democrat who would end the war and negotiate peace with the Confederates. When Lincoln won reelection, the South's fate looked even direr. Booth had not been a soldier during the war, which frustrated him, and his hatred of Lincoln and the North now convinced him to strike a blow.

Chapter 6: The Original Plan

Today, Booth's assassination of Lincoln is often the only part of the plot that Americans remember, but in November 1864, Booth's plan did not involve murder. When Lincoln brought General Ulysses S. Grant east and put him in charge of all armies, Grant, William Tecumseh Sherman (now in charge out west) and the Lincoln Administration changed their military policies to one that resembled total warfare. The North's great advantages in manpower and resources would now be more heavily relied upon to defeat the South. One of the most important changes was that the Union stopped exchanging prisoners of war, a move clearly designed to ensure that the Confederacy would be harder pressed to fill its armies. Originally, President Lincoln had opposed such exchanges, believing that giving wartime rights to the Confederacy implicitly acknowledged their independence, but they had been generally welcomed by both sides from almost the beginning of the war. Captives were exchanged and traded throughout the conflict's first few years. Exchanges were often not equal but were dependent on the rank of the soldiers being exchanged. For example, a captured general was exchanged for 46 privates. One major was worth eight privates, while a colonel was worth 15. The varying ranks of the soldiers, with privates at the bottom and generals at the top, allowed for different proportions of exchanges.

Ending the exchange eventually led to atrocities at prison camps like Andersonville and Camp Douglas in Illinois, but it had the desired effect of starving the South of able soldiers. Booth was particularly outraged by this, which many on both sides considered barbaric and contrary to the rules of warfare. In fact, generals on both sides still continued the exchange without informing their superiors.

It was this termination of prisoner exchanges that served as the motive for Booth's original plan. The North might not be willing to exchange soldiers, but Booth was sure they'd exchange for the President. Thus, Booth began gathering conspirators for a plot to kidnap President Lincoln and use him as a negotiating token to get back Confederate troops. Booth figured the President would be worth a great number of soldiers, which would give the rebels a potentially huge and much needed influx of men. A month before Lincoln's reelection in 1864, Booth took a trip to Montreal, which was a hotbed for Confederate espionage at the time, and he spent 10 days there. Historians are still unsure what exactly Booth did while he was there, but many have since speculated that he discussed kidnap plans with better connected members of the Confederate Secret Service and networks of spies.

Kidnap was still the plan when Lincoln's second inauguration took place on March 4, 1865. Despite his hatred of Lincoln, Booth attended the President's second inauguration in Washington. Along with a crowd of over 50,000 spectators, Booth watched as the President took the oath and now delivered his famous second inaugural address on the steps of the unfinished U.S. Capitol Building. Alongside Booth in the audience were several of his eventual co-conspirators: Samuel Arnold, George Atzerodt, David Herold, Michael O'Laughlen, Lewis Powell and John Surratt. All of the conspirators were either from or lived in the Washington, D.C. area or in Maryland, and all were opposed to President Lincoln and were fervent supporters of the Confederates. With the exception of George Atzerodt, who was born in Germany, all of the co-conspirators were Americans.

A picture of Lincoln's second inauguration. Booth is actually visible in the picture.

In the same month as the President's inauguration, Booth assembled this group of conspirators, which came together to discuss politics and the ongoing Civil War, as well as the kidnapping plot. Their most regular meeting place, and their most notorious, was the boarding house of Mary Surratt, a Southern sympathizer who would later be accused of facilitating Confederate espionage. Her son John was an active conspirator with Booth, and people staying at the boarding house would later tell military tribunals that Mary met with him as well.

1890 picture of Surratt's Boarding House

On March 15, the group met at Gautier's Restaurant at 252 Pennsylvania Avenue in Washington, just blocks from the White House. There, they discussed a plan to kidnap the President of the United States, send him to the Confederate capitol in Richmond, and hold him ransom until the Union released Confederate troops. Initially, the most realistic option for capturing the President would be to do so while he was in transit. This ensured that his security detail would be more limited than usual, and his travels were likely to be carried out in less densely populated places, ensuring minimal public awareness of the event. This would allow the group to scurry the President away to Richmond, where he could be held for ransom.

Two days later, on March 17, St. Patrick's Day, Booth learned that the President was going to head north to attend a play called *Still Waters Run Deep* at Campbell Military Hospital, located in the northern outskirts of Washington. Because Booth was a member of the nation's acting elite, he was privy to private information about public dignitaries, including the President, attending plays in the D.C. area, the very thing that made his plot possible the following month.

Booth informed his fellow conspirators, and they all agreed to go forward with the plan. Because the President's destination was known and his route could be reasonably assumed, the opportunity presented itself as the perfect one. The conspirators thus assembled along the President's route, hoping to intercept him along his way to the evening matinee. The sun was setting on Washington, providing cover to the conspirators in the darkened streets.

The conspirators were waiting for a man who would never show. To Booth's great dismay, the President had changed his mind and no longer planned to see *Still Waters Run Deep.* Instead, Lincoln attended a ceremony at National Hotel for the 140th Indiana Regiment, which was presenting its governor with a captured battle flag. Ironically, Booth was living at that very hotel at the time.

Chapter 7: From Kidnap to Murder

With the passing of March, the Civil War had seen critical developments. General Grant and the Army of the Potomac had been laying siege to Robert E. Lee's Army of Northern Virginia at Petersburg since June 1864, gradually stretching Lee's lines and inching their way toward the Confederacy's main railroad hub, which was only miles away from Richmond itself.

Lee's siege lines at Petersburg were finally broken on April 1 at the Battle of Five Forks, which is best remembered for General George Pickett enjoying a cod bake lunch while his men were being defeated. Historians have attributed it to unusual environmental acoustics that prevented Pickett and his staff from hearing the battle despite their close proximity, not that it mattered to the Confederates at the time, and that would have been Pickett's most famous role in the Civil War if not for the charge named after him on the final day of the Battle of Gettysburg.

When the siege lines were broken at Petersburg, that city fell the following day, as Lee began a week long retreat that famously ended with his surrender at Appomattox Court House. On April 3, the Confederate capitol of Richmond fell to Union troops, and days later President Lincoln himself entered the city and even sat at the desk in the Confederate Executive Mansion where Confederate President Jefferson Davis had led the South for nearly the entire war. This was also a significant development for Booth's plot though, because Richmond had been the intended destination to bring Lincoln after the conspirators kidnapped him. Now, to Booth's horror, the President was in Richmond of his own accord. With the city under Union control, where could they bring the President?

Developments in prisoner exchanges had also prompted more fundamental questions among the conspirators. In early 1865, General Grant agreed to resume prisoner exchanges on a man-for-man basis, believing the war was nearing its end. He intended to negotiate exchanges until all prisoners from both sides were released. Capturing the President had intended to serve as a negotiating piece in discussions over prisoner exchanges, which General Grant had earlier stopped. With exchanges resumed, what purpose was there in kidnapping Lincoln?

The Old Soldiers Home, where the conspirators planned to kidnap Lincoln

Booth's original plan now lay in shambles, and all of the conspirators were now compelled to reconsider their purpose. Richmond was no longer a viable place to take the President, there was no obvious reason to take the President at all since prisoner exchanges were back in action, and the war was clearly nearing its end. Kidnapping the President would do nothing to bring the Confederacy back into existence or save slavery in the South.

Booth didn't care, continuing to hold out hope of a Confederate victory. To understand Booth's rationale, it is important to remember that General Joseph E. Johnston, who Lee famously replaced at the head of the Army of Northern Virginia, still had a sizable army opposing General Sherman's army near the Carolinas. Although Appomattox is generally regarded as the end of the Civil War, there were still tens of thousands of Confederates in the field throughout April 1865, and Jefferson Davis himself was still holding out hope while fleeing from Richmond. Thus, Booth still intended to help the Confederacy somehow.

Two days after Appomattox, Lincoln gave a speech at the White House in which he expressed his desire to give former slaves the right to vote, a policy that would come to fruition through the 13th, 14th, and 15th Amendments. Naturally, such a policy infuriated Southerners, and Booth was so enraged by the speech that he was later alleged to have claimed, "Now, by God, I'll put him through. That is the last speech he will ever give."

On April 11, the other conspirators still believed the conspiracy was about kidnapping Lincoln, and there was dissension in the ranks. Samuel Arnold and Michael O'Laughlen informed Booth of their intention to not participate in any kidnapping of the President. For them, the resumption of the prisoner exchange program and the coming end of the war made holding the President for ransom a moot point. They chose to disassociate themselves of the entire conspiracy.

Everyone else was still on board, but the group as a whole needed to regroup. Kidnapping the President made less sense than it had before, but these conspirators agreed that something still needed to be done. Various plans were thrown around, including John Surratt's thought that blowing up the White House with a bomb would be the easiest and most effective method of dealing with the President. Surratt had connections with Confederate bomb-making experts who he thought could mine the White House and destroy it. This unlikely plot was made even more unlikely when Thomas Harney, the Confederacy's bomb expert who Surratt considered most likely to successfully bomb the White House, was captured by Union forces on April 10.

While Surratt was in Montreal, likely networking with Confederate spies, Booth and the remaining conspirators were still in Washington. Together they devised a more feasible, though also more complicated, plan to assassinate high-ranking members of the federal government. It would take a miracle to save the South, and they figured the chaos that would ensue with a leaderless national government might do the trick. On April 13, Booth and the conspirators met at the Surratt Boarding House and hatched a plan to assassinate Lincoln, Vice President Andrew Johnson, and Secretary of State William Seward, a sinister plot they thought would throw the federal government into disarray at a critical moment in its history.

Given the manner in which the plot changed, it's not surprising that the conspiracy was still riddled with glaring errors. For whatever reason, the plot overlooked Secretary of War Edwin Stanton, who in many respects asserted the most authority in the wake of Lincoln's assassination before the government began functioning normally again. And Booth pegged conspirator George Atzerodt to be the one to kill Vice President Johnson, even after Atzerodt objected to the murder plots and asked out of the conspiracy.

Now that the conspirators had their new plot, they still needed to figure out when they would carry it out. As fate would have it, they didn't have long to wait.

Atzerodt

Chapter 8: April 14-15, 1865

One of the most decisive days in American history began for Booth at midnight, who found himself wide awake lying in bed. In his diary entry for the day, Booth wrote, "Our cause being almost lost, something decisive and great must be done." But when he woke up, Booth himself was unaware that the plot would be carried out that night.

Lincoln, on the other hand, slept more than usual. The day was Good Friday, and it was one of the first days in many years that Lincoln was relatively stress-free. Though he still had plenty of work to do, its urgency paled in comparison to the decisions he had had to make during the war. After the capture of Richmond and Appomattox, Lincoln now focused more on how to reconstruct the nation than winning the war. At around 8:00 a.m., the President and his son ate breakfast together at a leisurely pace.

Later that morning, he met with many dignitaries to discuss logistics about Reconstruction. He met with Speaker of the House Schuyler Colfax, General Grant, the Governor of Maryland and Senator Creswell, also of Maryland. At 11:00 a.m., the President held a special Cabinet Meeting with General Grant in attendance. Grant relayed intimate details of the surrender at Appomattox to the Cabinet, and the Cabinet discussed what to do about Confederate leaders now that the war had been won. Lincoln hoped they would simply flee the country. Either way, he thought good news was to come, telling his Cabinet that he had a dream the previous night in which he was flying away in some sort of vessel at an indescribable speed. He had had this dream before major victories in the war, and thought it was a harbinger of positive developments. General Grant, on the other hand, reminded the President that many of the other times the President reported the dream, the Union had lost battles. The President remarked to his Cabinet that, either way, something big was going to happen. Cabinet officials would later note how unusually happy Lincoln was, with Secretary of the Treasury Hugh McCulloch noting, "I never saw Mr. Lincoln so cheerful and happy."

At the end of the meeting, around 2:00 p.m., President Lincoln asked both General Grant and Secretary of War Stanton if they would like to join the Lincoln's at Ford's Theatre later that evening. As it turned out, Stanton and Grant were hearing about Lincoln's plan for the night after Booth had already learned it. Both declined the offer, but Lincoln had already conveyed his plan to bring Grant that night to the people at Ford's Theatre. When Booth stopped by the theater at noon to pick up mail from his permanent mailbox, owner John Ford's brother casually mentioned the president would be attending *Our American Cousin* that night, a play Booth knew so well that he later timed his shooting of Lincoln in conjunction with the play's funniest line, which Booth figured would help him because it would draw the loudest laughs.

Now Booth was set on killing Lincoln during the play. That afternoon he arranged with Mary Surratt to have a package delivered to her tavern in Maryland. Booth had previously stored guns and ammunition at the tavern, and he asked Surratt to inform one of her tenants to have those ready for him to pick up there. It would be this meeting that doomed Mary Surratt to her fate of becoming the first woman executed by the federal government.

After some paperwork, Lincoln and Mary Todd went for a carriage ride throughout the capital, enjoying the fresh air and relaxing environment for nearly two hours. When they returned to the White House, they asked Illinois Governor Richard Oglesby if he wanted to join them at Ford's Theater. He, too, declined. Ultimately, Major Henry Rathbone and his fiancée Clara Harris, the daughter of a New York Senator, accepted the invitation and became Lincoln's guests in the presidential box that night.

Rathbone

At 7:00 p.m., Booth and the other conspirators convened to put the plot in motion. Lewis Powell, a rough and tumble veteran who had suffered a battle wound at Gettysburg, was to break into Secretary of State Seward's home, accompanied by David Herold. There, they were to assassinate the Secretary, who was still weak and recovering from wounds he had suffered in a carriage accident. The same evening, George Atzerodt was to head to the Kirkwood Hotel, where Vice President Johnson was living, and assassinate him as well. All of the attacks were to take place simultaneously around 10:00 p.m., and the conspirators agreed on an escape spot in Maryland to meet up after the attacks.

Herold

Between 8:00 and 8:30, the Lincoln's left the White House, and arrived at Ford's Theater shortly thereafter. They were late for the play, which began at 8:00 p.m. A special box on the second story balcony was decorated for the President's arrival, and the Lincolns, Major Rathbone, and Clara Harris settled into their spots and enjoyed the show. They were initially guarded by a policeman, John Frederick Parker, but for reasons that are still unclear, Parker left his post during the middle of the play and headed to a tavern with Lincoln's coachman.

When Booth had heard Grant was attending the play, either he or O'Laughlen followed Grant, who was boarding a train to head to Philadelphia, not Ford's Theatre. It's believed that O'Laughlen attempted to attack Grant that night, but Grant and his wife were too heavily protected by staff onboard the train, and the car they were riding in was locked.

Often lost in the aftermath of Lincoln's assassination is Lewis Powell's unbelievable attack on Secretary of State Seward. In fact, Powell's attack on Seward was the first attack of the night. On the other side of Washington D.C., Seward was in his home still convalescing from a carriage accident on April 5 that left him with a concussion, a broken jaw and a broken arm. One of the most famous aspects of the attack was that Seward was wearing a neck brace, but in fact doctors had put together a splint to help his jaw repair.

Seward

Powell

Shortly after 10:00 p.m., Powell, dressed as a pharmacist and carrying a revolver and a Bowie knife, knocked on the door of Seward's home. The butler answered the knock, at which point Powell told the butler he needed to speak with the Secretary personally, to instruct him how to take his medication.

The butler let him in, but as soon as he entered, Seward's son Frederick stopped him. Not recognizing Powell, Frederick told him Seward was sleeping and could not be awoken, but just as he said that, Seward's daughter opened a door and told them the Secretary was awake. Powell now knew his location, pointed a gun at Frederick's head, and fired. Luckily, the gun misfired, and after the burly Civil War veteran bludgeoned Frederick with the gun and knocked him out cold, the gun was broken.

Powell wouldn't be able to shoot Seward, but he still had the Bowie knife. After knocking out Frederick, Powell rushed wildly into Seward's room and began stabbing at Seward's neck and face, knocking him out of the bed and onto the floor. When Seward's daughter screamed, it awoke Seward's other son, Augustus. Together with the sergeant on detail there, the two began wrestling with Powell, who still managed to stab them and Seward's daughter as they tried to fight him off.

After stabbing those three, Powell fled the scene, only to run directly into a messenger with a telegram at the door. Powell stabbed him in the back and exited the house, only to find that co-conspirator David Herold had abandoned him and fled when he heard the commotion coming from the house. Powell left the scene on horseback, but he had no clue how to get to the meeting spot in Maryland and instead began hiding out in Washington D.C.

Seward had been badly wounded, but not fatally. The jaw splint had deflected Powell's stabs away from the jugular vein, and Seward would go on to recover.

While Secretary of State Seward was under attack, Ford's Theater was in still in the middle of *Our American Cousin*. Booth had suggested the attacks take place around 10:00, but he entered the theater just before 10:30. Because he was a well-known and widely admired actor, no one thought twice about letting him in. Admissions simply assumed he was interested in viewing the play. Moreover, nobody would have thought twice about granting Booth access to Lincoln's presidential box, even if the guard had been in his proper position.

Just at 10:30, the play was at Act III, Scene II, and the actor Harry Hawk was alone on the stage when a gunshot echoed across the theater. The President's bodyguard was absent, having ambled across the street to the nearby tavern. Without having to worry about the bodyguard, Booth was able to penetrate the double-doors of the President's box easily, and he barricaded the first door behind him with a stick so that the President could not escape.

Booth knew *Our American Cousin* by heart, having seen it numerous times. He waited between the doors until Hawk uttered the funniest line of the play. When the audience erupted in laughter, Booth made his shot, striking the President in the back of the head. The President slumped forward, and Mary immediately began screaming while grabbing the back of his shirt.

The pistol Booth used.

At this time, Mary Lincoln, Rathbone and Clara Harris were still the only ones who were aware the president had been shot. As Lincoln slumped forward, Rathbone lunged at Booth to try to stop him, but Booth pulled out his knife and stabbed Rathbone twice before jumping out of the balcony down to the stage, about 12 feet below. It is widely believed that Booth suffered a broken left leg during the jump when his foot got entangled in the flag decorating the box. Always the showman, Booth got up to his feet, crossed the stage, and reportedly yelled "Sic semper tyrannis", which was Virginia's state motto and Latin for "thus always to tyrants."

The crowd was still in a state of confusion while Booth made his last appearance on stage, but Mary and Rathbone were yelling out "catch that man," at which point the audience realized that the excitement was not part of the play. Some members ran towards Booth, but no one was able to capture him, and Booth was able to hop onto the horse he had waiting for him outside and escape.

Having likely suffered a broken leg, Booth knew his part of the assassination plot hadn't gone directly according to plan, but he had no way of knowing just how poorly the rest of it had gone. Herold and Powell had been separated, with Powell failing to kill Seward, but even that was more of a success than George Atzerodt's attack on Vice President Andrew Johnson. This is because that attack never took place. Atzerodt, who Booth insisted on tabbing for the attack on Johnson despite his objections to murder, had lost his nerve while drinking at the Kirkwood's hotel bar. Instead, the drunk Atzerodt roamed the city's streets that night, but only after he had asked the bartender about Johnson, which obviously drew suspicion when news of the attacks on Lincoln and Seward spread. The next day, police searched the room Atzerodt had booked and found a revolver and Bowie knife.

After the shooting, a doctor in the audience named Charles Leale rushed towards the President's box, only to find that Booth had sealed the door. Together with another doctor in the audience, Charles Sabin Taft, the two men assessed the President's state. He had no pulse, and at first Leale believed him to be dead. The two doctors unbuttoned the President's shirt to try to find the bullet hole before discovering the bullet had entered the back of the President's head. Leale removed blood clots from the hole, which helped Lincoln start to breathe better.

Regardless, both doctors immediately believed the President's wound was mortal and that he would not recover. The two men, together with another Doctor Albert King, consulted on the state of the President. They agreed it was best for him to die in comfort, and not in the box in the theater. However, a bumpy carriage ride back to the White House, which would almost certainly draw a crowd, was not a reasonable option.

The three doctors and some soldiers in the audience carried the President's body across the street, where Henry Safford told them the President could stay in his residence. A bed was prepared, though the President was too tall and needed to lay on it diagonally. At this point, the Petersen House became the de facto headquarters for the federal government and the manhunt for Booth, who had already been immediately identified as the assassin by the time he exited the theater.

The Petersen House

Presidential physicians, including the Surgeon General and Lincoln's personal doctor, arrived to assess the state of the President. They all agreed that the President would not survive.

At this point, news of the shooting began to spread, with Secretary of the Navy Gideon Welles and Secretary of War Stanton rushing over to the Petersen House to all but take control of the federal government. Understandably, Lincoln's wife Mary was a complete wreck, sobbing so loudly that Stanton at one point ordered people to remove her from the room. Indeed, when they arrived, the situation was as grave as they were told, and doctors thought the President would survive for only a few more hours. Physicians, including Canada's first African-American doctor, Anderson Ruffin Abbott, continued to work on the President throughout the night, but the hemorrhaging of his brain could not be stopped.

The following morning, at 7:22 a.m., President Lincoln died, surrounded by Senator Charles Sumner, Generals Henry Halleck, Richard Oglesby and Montgomery Meigs, and Secretary of War Stanton. Mary was not present; she was too distressed throughout the night to see the President. As Lincoln took his last breath, legend has it Stanton famously said, "Now he belongs to the ages." (Other historians speculate he said, "Now he belongs to the angels.")

Stanton

Chapter 9: The Manhunt for Booth

SURRAT.   BOOTH.   HAROLD.

War Department, Washington, April 20, 1865,

 # $100,000 REWARD!

THE MURDERER

Of our late beloved President, Abraham Lincoln,

IS STILL AT LARGE.

$50,000 REWARD

Will be paid by this Department for his apprehension, in addition to any reward offered by Municipal Authorities or State Executives.

$25,000 REWARD

Will be paid for the apprehension of JOHN H. SURRATT, one of Booth's Accomplices.

$25,000 REWARD

Will be paid for the apprehension of David C. Harold, another of Booth's accomplices.

LIBERAL REWARDS will be paid for any information that shall conduce to the arrest of either of the above-named criminals, or their accomplices.

All persons harboring or secreting the said persons, or either of them, or aiding or assisting their concealment or escape, will be treated as accomplices in the murder of the President and the attempted assassination of the Secretary of State, and shall be subject to trial before a Military Commission and the punishment of DEATH.

Let the stain of innocent blood be removed from the land by the arrest and punishment of the murderers.

All good citizens are exhorted to aid public justice on this occasion. Every man should consider his own conscience charged with this solemn duty, and rest neither night nor day until it be accomplished.

EDWIN M. STANTON, Secretary of War.

DESCRIPTIONS.—BOOTH is Five Feet 7 or 8 inches high, slender build, high forehead, black hair, black eyes, and wears a heavy black moustache.

JOHN H. SURRAT is about 5 feet, 9 inches. Hair rather thin and dark; eyes rather light; no beard. Would weigh 145 or 150 pounds. Complexion rather pale and clear, with color in his cheeks. Wore light clothes of fine quality. Shoulders square; cheek bones rather prominent; chin narrow; ears projecting at the top; forehead rather low and square, but broad. Parts his hair on the right side; neck rather long. His lips are firmly set. A slim man.

DAVID C. HAROLD is five feet six inches high, hair dark, eyes dark, eyebrows rather heavy, full face, nose short, hand short and fleshy, feet small, instep high, round bodied, naturally quick and active, slightly closes his eyes when looking at a person.

NOTICE.—In addition to the above, State and other authorities have offered rewards amounting to almost one hundred thousand dollars, making an aggregate of about TWO HUNDRED THOUSAND DOLLARS.

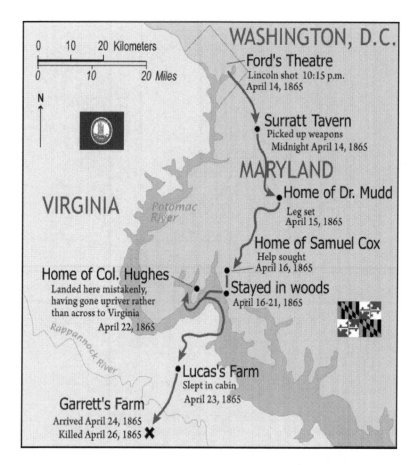

Booth's and Herold's Escape Route

Given the lack of technology and the delays caused by the shock of Lincoln's assassination, the manhunt for Booth and the unraveling of the conspiracy occurred extremely quickly. Much of the conspiracy was done in by bumbling errors made by the men who didn't escape, while the manhunt for Booth was greatly aided by his broken leg. It is widely believed that Booth suffered a broken leg jumping from the presidential box after shooting Lincoln. If not, it's likely that he suffered a broken leg during the ride out of Washington. Either way, what is clear is that Booth was hampered by a broken leg before the night of April 14 ended.

Despite being in great pain that made horseback riding nearly unbearable, Booth managed to escape as planned to Maryland shortly after the shooting. So did David Herold, who had left Powell at Seward's house while Powell was still trying to kill the Secretary of State. The two met up at Mary Surratt's tavern in Surrattville, Maryland, where they picked up supplies, including a revolver, to assist in their escape. These included the materials Booth had told Mrs. Surratt to ensure would be there.

From there, the two continued southward to the home of a Dr. Samuel Mudd, where they arrived at about 4:00 a.m. on April 15. The doctor set Booth's fractured leg in a cast, and he furnished Booth with crutches. Controversy still exists today over the extent of Mudd's involvement in Booth's escape, and whether he was an unwitting plan or had foreknowledge of Booth's conspiracy. Although it is known that Mudd and Booth knew each other dating back to 1864, Mudd proclaimed his innocence until his death, but Atzerodt later told federal investigators that Mudd knew about the plot ahead of time. Either way, Mudd waited until Sunday, April 16, to get word to authorities that Booth and Herold had been there, which ultimately made investigators suspicious.

Within hours of the assassination, Secretary of War Stanton began coordinating the manhunt with authorities. In addition to posting a $100,000 reward for the capture of Booth and his co-conspirators, federal troops had dispersed across Maryland and northern Virginia in search of them, while an investigation of accomplices ensued in Washington.

After spending more than half of April 15 at Dr. Mudd's home, Booth and Herold hid in the swamps and woods of rural Maryland along their escape route to the South. The following day, they made it to the home of a mutual friend, Samuel Cox, in southern Maryland, who helped them contact Thomas Jones. Jones was a Confederate spy who agreed to assist the two in navigating their escape. From there, Jones escorted the two through the woods of southern Maryland from April 16-21, but they did not travel much distance in that time, which would prove crucial because the manhunt was bearing down on them. Booth's injury had made traveling great distances too difficult.

Once the two crossed the Potomac, they crossed the farmland of Virginia, settling down in various farms along the route. By April 24, 10 days after the assassination, the pair made it to Garrett's farm. Incredibly, the family was still unaware of Lincoln's assassination, making it possible for Booth to convince the family that he was an injured Confederate soldier who had trekked through the woods of Virginia for days in search of help.

Garrett Farmhouse

Unbeknownst to them, federal authorities were closing in on them. The manhunt naturally assumed that Booth would be heading south from Washington D.C., where he would be more likely to find sympathizers and aid in the Southern states. When they found out Mudd had set his leg, it confirmed a southern route.

Still, the federal authorities and soldiers pursuing Booth had no clue where he was on April 25. Lieutenant Edward P. Doherty, who was leading the 16th New York Cavalry, later wrote in his official report that they only "had reliable information that the assassin Booth and his accomplice were somewhere between the Potomac and Rappahannock Rivers." That day, while interrogating men near a ferry spot, the 16th New York Cavalry learned that men matching Booth's and Herold's descriptions had crossed via that very ferry the day before on their way to the house of a Mr. Roland. Moreover, they learned that Booth and Herold had tried to hire someone to take them to Bowling Green, which as it turned out was 12 miles away from Garrett's Farm.

Booth met his fate early on the morning of April 26, when Doherty's unit of about 30 men surrounded Garrett's Farm and quickly learned from Mr. Garrett that Booth and Herold were in the barn. Doherty explained what happened in his official report:

"Sergt. Boston Corbett, Company L, Sixteenth New York Cavalry asked permission to enter the barn alone, which I refused. Booth all this time was very defiant and refused to surrender. At one time he said if we would draw up in line fifty paces off he would come out, adding that he was lame and had only one leg. This, however, I refused. Booth up to this time had denied there was anyone in the barn besides himself. Considerable conversation now took place between myself, Booth, and the detectives. We threatened to burn the barn if he did not surrender; at one time gave him ten minutes to make up his mind. Finally, Booth said, "Oh; Captain, there is a man here who wants to surrender awful bad:" I answered, and I think Mr. Baker did at the same time, "Hand out your arms." Herold replied, "I have none." Baker said, "We know exactly what you have got." Booth replied, "I own all the arms, and intend to use them on you gentlemen."... Almost simultaneous with my taking Herold out of the barn the hay in the rear of the barn was ignited by Mr. Conger, and the barn fired. Sergt. Boston Corbett, Company L, Sixteenth New York Cavalry, shot the assassin Booth, wounding him in the neck. I entered the barn as soon as the shot was fired, dragging Herold with me, and found that Booth had fallen on his back. Messrs. Conger and Baker, with some of my men, entered the barn and took hold of Booth."

The unit had orders not to kill Booth, so the soldiers lit the corners of the barn on fire in order to smoke Booth out. However, when Sergeant Boston Corbett spotted Booth near the back door of the barn holding two guns, he mortally wounded Booth with a shot to the spine. Booth spent the next two hours paralyzed, and shortly before his death, he asked a soldier to hold up his hands. Looking at his hands, Booth uttered his last words, "Useless. Useless."

Although they had intended to take Booth alive, Doherty wrote, "I beg to state that it has afforded my command and myself inexpressible pleasure to be the humble instruments of capturing the foul assassins who caused the death of our beloved President and plunged the nation in mourning." Corbett was actually placed under arrest for disobeying orders, but the charges were dropped at the behest of Secretary of War Stanton himself. Each member of the 16th New York Cavalry collected a share of the reward for Booth's death, receiving over $1,500 each. Over the coming decades, Corbett was so volatile and unstable that he was eventually placed in an insane asylum in the 1880s.

Corbett

Booth's belongings found with him when he was captured and killed.

Amazingly, despite being the only one instantly identified as one of the conspirators, and despite being killed less than two weeks after the assassination, Booth was the last of the main conspirators to be captured. It took federal soldiers 12 days to capture Booth and Herold, but it took far less time for Powell and Atzerodt to literally walk themselves into custody.

On the night of April 14, while his co-conspirators were carrying out their attacks and fleeing, George Atzerodt was stumbling around. Atzerodt was supposed to assassinate Vice President (now President) Andrew Johnson, but he got so drunk that he spent the nights walking throughout the city. Apparently, he never spent any part of the night in the hotel room he had booked. However, when Atzerodt asked the bartender where Vice President Johnson was sleeping, the curious question would lead authorities straight to him.

The bartender contacted the police, who were now fully engaged in a city-wide manhunt and investigation. The following day, the military police searched Atzerodt's room, finding a revolver and a bank book belonging to Booth. This was sufficient evidence to warrant arresting Atzerodt. On April 20, George Atzerodt was arrested without a fight, in Germantown, Maryland, where he had been staying with his cousin since leaving the hotel.

Meanwhile, Powell unwittingly unraveled the rest of the conspiracy for authorities. After attacking the Secretary of State, Powell exited the home to find that his accomplice, David Herold, had already fled. Powell was now being chased by Seward's family and neighbors, so he fled the scene on horseback, leaving his weapons behind. Powell fled to a cemetery in a Washington suburb, where he discarded remaining evidence and remained for some time. He hid in a tree there for three days, aware that he was being chased, but unsure of the route to the agreed-upon Maryland meeting location.

Obviously Powell knew he could not hide out in public forever, but without having any clue how to get to a safe place in Maryland, the only viable location he could think of was the boarding house of Mary Surratt, where the conspirators had met on so many occasions.

Powell could not have picked a worse time than the evening of April 17 to reappear at Mary Surratt's boarding house. Through a combination of factors, including the information relayed through Surratt's African-American servants, federal authorities tied Surratt's son John to the attempt on Seward, and they came to believe Mary Surratt was somehow involved in the plot. The boarding house's association with Booth had been attested to by witnesses as well.

When authorities entered her home, Mary denied having any involvement in the plot. She also lied about her son's whereabouts and the fact she had helped Booth arrange to pick up a package at her tavern on April 14. On the night of April 17, as authorities were getting ready to charge her for the conspiracy, Powell showed up at her door in disguise, claiming he was there to dig a ditch. Mary claimed not to recognize Powell, but not surprisingly, the authorities did not believe Powell was there to dig a ditch at night. And given how often Powell was at the boarding house, Mary's claim not to recognize him struck the authorities as yet another lie. Both Powell and Surratt were arrested that night.

Ironically, Mary suffered a far worse fate than her son, despite the fact he was almost certainly more involved in the conspiracy. John Surratt Jr. also proved to be far more difficult to catch. At the time of the assassination, he was in Elmira, New York, nowhere near Washington, D.C. However, interrogations of arrested conspirators led authorities to believe he was involved in the plot. By then, he had fled to Montreal, Canada, where he was protected by Roman Catholic priests.

Surratt didn't just seek safety north of the border. Eventually, he fled overseas to England, where he assumed the name John Watson. From there, he became nomadic, moving around Europe and North Africa, while federal authorities maintained a warrant for his arrest. He even served briefly in the army of the Papal States, but in November 1866, more than a year after the murder, an old American friend traveling through Italy recognized Surratt and alerted the American Embassy. He was arrested on November 7, and sent to an Italian prison, but managed to escape, and fled to Alexandria, Egypt, where he was again arrested by U.S. authorities on November 23. He was sent home via ship to Washington, D.C., where he was imprisoned in early 1867.

In addition to the conspirators most directly involved in the assassination of the President and the attempted assassinations of Secretary of State Seward and Vice President Johnson, dozens more were arrested on related charges, though many were later released.

Two of the original conspirators, Samuel Arnold and Michael O'Laughlen, were both arrested, despite backing out of the plot when it turned into an assassination scheme. Arnold was arrested in Fortress Monroe, Virginia, after authorities found correspondence between him and Booth that pertained to a plot against the government. Arnold proved especially critical to the government, as he had backed out of the plot and was willing to give extensive information to authorities. This information led them to another former conspirator, Michael O'Laughlen. He voluntarily surrendered himself in Baltimore.

In addition to Mary Surratt and Powell, several other important arrests were made on April 17. Among them was Edman Spangler, a Ford's Theatre employee who held Booth's horse in the back of the theater so that the assassin could make an easy escape. The owner of the theater himself, John Ford, was arrested as a suspicious character. A boarder at Surratt's home, and Booth's own brother were also incarcerated. Many others who were tangentially connected to the supply chain of the assassination and escape were arrested, including the stable owner who sold Booth a horse, Dr. Mudd, Samuel Cox and Thomas Jones, who had helped Herold and Booth escape through Maryland and Virginia.

Chapter 10: Trying the Conspirators

The killing of Booth and the apprehension of the conspiracy's main players was remarkably successful, but the means of trying the conspirators, and who to try for what, was an open question among military officials. The events were intimately connected to the Civil War, but they were also carried out by civilians independent of any military body. And though the authorities tried desperately to see if there was a connection between the assassination and the upper reaches of the Confederate government (including the recently captured Jefferson Davis), the inability to find hard evidence connecting Booth to actual Confederates ensured the way to try the people caught was heavily debated. For example, Secretary of War Stanton supported a military tribunal to be followed by executions, but former Attorney General Lincoln Bates favored a civilian trial, believing a military tribunal was unconstitutional given the circumstances.

In the aftermath of Lincoln's death, members of the government worried that a military tribunal and execution of Lincoln's assassins would turn *them* into martyrs. In the long run, it didn't. While the South was not traumatized at all by Lincoln's passing, they were not eager to laud the plot against the federal government. To many, even in the South, Booth's and the conspirators' actions were dishonorable. The South recognized that it had lost, and Booth's actions were viewed as a foolish attempt to save the Confederacy.

To resolve the issue, President Johnson asked sitting Attorney General James Speed to prepare a reasoned brief defending his position on the issue. Speed reasoned that, because the President was assassinated before the complete cessation of the Confederate rebellion, the issue was properly handled by the war department, as it was an act of war against the United States. A military tribunal was thus decided. On May 1, 1865, President Johnson ordered a nine-person military tribunal be set up to try to the alleged assassins. The members of the commission were: Generals David Hunter, August Kautz, Albion Howe, James Ekin, David Clendenin, Lewis Wallace, Robert Foster, T.M. Harris and Colonel C.H. Tomkins.

Holding military tribunals greatly affected the ability of the conspirators to defend themselves. The rules of the commission stipulated that a simple majority vote would lead to a conviction, while a vote of two-thirds or more meant the death penalty. All conspirators were offered legal counsel, if they wanted it, but the tribunal did not assure them basic trial rights afforded by the Constitution either. In particular, evidence like hearsay that would never be admissible in regular trial courts was allowed in the military tribunal.

Ultimately, only eight conspirators were charged and tried by the military tribunal: Samuel Arnold, George Atzerodt, David Herold, Samuel Mudd, Michael O'Laughlen, Lewis Powell, Edman Spangler and Mary Surratt. The trials began on May 9, 1865, and lasted for seven weeks, ending on June 30th, 1865. It was held on the third floor of the Old Arsenal Penitentiary.

Library of Congress
Photograph of the District penitentiary, about 1865, after it had been taken over by the United States Army for use as an arsenal.

The prosecution team charged with trying to convict the eight consisted of General Joseph Holt, John A. Bingham and HL Burnett, lawyers.

Lewis Powell's trial was the most convincing, since the assassin failed to kill his target and was witnessed by many in the Secretary of State's family. Additionally, the circumstances of his arrest added further evidence against him. Authorities had eye-witness reports against Powell, and he left guns and other belongings behind on his escape route. The best his defense attorney could do was to argue that his life not be taken because he was an insane fanatic. Regardless, Powell was found guilty and sentenced to death by hanging.

The evidence against David Herold was just as incriminating. He was, after all, apprehended in the company of Lincoln's assassin, John Wilkes Booth. Worse, Herold was proud of the crime, and bragged about it throughout the proceedings. His attorney had little hope for saving his client's life, and relied on the argument that Herold was a simpleton, too stupid to realize the gravity of his crime, and that his life should therefore be spared. The military tribunal didn't buy the argument and sentenced Herold to death by hanging.

The remaining defendants were not so easily prosecuted. George Atzerodt had not killed anyone, and explicitly said he was not interested in doing the job. Regardless, his hotel room showed correspondence with Booth and he had a gun under his pillow, suggesting he second-guessed his reluctance to kill the Vice President. His defense attorney used his cowardice to try to prevent Atzerodt from receiving the death penalty, noting his client was too cowardly to ever go through with the assassination. However, Atzerodt also took no active steps to stop the murder conspiracy despite his knowledge of it, and he went on the run after April 14 and hid out. The military tribunal eventually decided that he, too, deserved death by hanging.

Mary Surratt

Mary Surratt was the last and most controversial defendant to receive a conviction of death by hanging. Just about everyone believed she facilitated the conspiracy in critical ways, from the use of the boarding house to ensuring Booth could pick up supplies from her tavern, but did she know the intent of the conspiracy or play an active enough role to warrant death? Her culpability was rarely doubted, but she was among the most hotly defended. More witnesses testified on her behalf than any other defendant, and due to the nature of her involvement aiding and abetting the assassins, hers was a more evidence-intensive trial. The government relied on witnesses to attest that she had conspired with the assassins, including being present in meetings held by Booth and the other major conspirators. Meanwhile, her attorneys tried to portray Surratt as a woman loyal to the Union, who would not support killing the President. They also tried to impeach the testimony of the people who testified against her, including neighbors and servants, and knock out their testimony as unreliable. However, all of these defenses were undermined by the fact that, in the moments of her arrest, Powell came to her home with weapons and a clear intent to hide out. And her claim that she did not recognize Powell that night, despite the fact he had frequently met other conspirators in her boarding house, greatly damaged her believability. Although Powell would tell authorities Surratt was completely innocent, Atzerodt told authorities she was more deeply involved in the conspiracy than even authorities believed. Eventually she was thus convicted and sentenced to death by hanging. When President Johnson signed her death warrant, he is said to have remarked she "kept the nest that hatched the egg".

The remaining four defendants did not receive death sentences. Dr. Samuel Mudd, who set Booth's broken leg, was charged with aiding Booth in his escape. His defense focused on Mudd's being a Union man who treated his slaves well. Others testified against this, arguing that Mudd was indeed a Confederate sympathizer. Even still, authorities could prove no connection to the conspiracy other than the fact Mudd helped an injured Booth in the middle of the night on April 15, not exactly the most damning evidence. Mudd barely escaped the hangman, avoiding the death penalty by one vote, and was instead sentenced to life in prison. His guilt, however, was endlessly doubted, until President Johnson pardoned the doctor on March 8, 1869, in part because he had served ably as a doctor during a yellow fever outbreak at the prison in Fort Jefferson.

Dr. Mudd

Samuel Arnold's and Michael O'Laughlen's trials were very similar to the prior ones pertaining to aiding and abetting the assassins. Because they did not directly participate in the attacks, their trials focused on their loyalty to the Union and reluctance to kill. Those defenses spared them the death penalty, but not life in prison. Like Mudd, Arnold was pardoned in 1869, but O'Laughlen died of yellow fever in 1867 while at Fort Jefferson.

Finally, Edmund Spangler, who had watched Booth's horse while he shot the President, was given the lightest sentence of the eight, at six years in prison. The evidence against him was highly questionable, as many were uncertain that he knew the purpose of watching Booth's horse was to kill the President. Spangler allegedly thought the horse was poorly tamed, and simply needed someone to keep an eye on it. Because of this, he was only sentenced to six years in prison. He served a shorter sentence, however, when President Johnson also pardoned him in 1869.

Because the eight had been sentenced by military tribunal, the Commander-in-Chief needed to give his ultimate seal of approval before action could be taken. When the trial ended in June, the Commission forwarded its report to President Johnson, who signed the death warrants. It marked the first time a woman had been sentenced the death penalty by the U.S. government, a step that alarmed even some of the judges of the tribunal, who asked Johnson to commute Surratt's death sentence.

Mary Surratt's lawyers hurried together a review to be done in lower courts, but President Johnson quashed the review, saying that a military tribunal sentence could not be appealed in civilian courts.

On July 7, 1865, Union General Winfield Scott Hancock brought the four convicted assassins to the Old Arsenal Penitentiary in Washington, D.C., around noon. At 1:30, the trap underneath the hanging four was removed, and Mary Surratt, George Atzerodt, Lewis Powell and David Herold fell to their deaths.

The death warrants are read before the hangings.

The execution of Mary Surratt, Powell, Herold, and Atzerodt

In August 1867, John Surratt was brought back to the United States from Egypt, where he was tried in a civilian court. The jury was hung on his case, and he was thus not guilty. He was released from prison and began a speaking tour, detailing the conspiracy across the nation. Despite almost certainly being more involved in the conspiracy than his mother, Surratt lived out the rest of his life a free man.

Apart from Michael O'Laughlen, who died in prison, the remaining conspirators were released by President Johnson in an eleventh hour pardon before he left office in early 1869. The President's pardons outraged the North. Not only did he pardon the assassins, but he also pardoned high-ranking members of the Confederacy, and offered excessive clemency.

Chapter 11: The Aftermath and Legacy of the Lincoln Assassination

Abraham Lincoln was not the first president to die in office, nor the first president to be shot at (an assassin tried to kill President Andrew Jackson nearly 30 years earlier), but he was the first American President to be assassinated.

After the President's death, his body was moved to the White House, where he lay in state in a temporary coffin. There, the President's body was prepared for burial. A public viewing took place from 9:30 a.m. until 5:30 p.m. on April 18th, which was followed by a private viewing for two hours afterwards. A short, private service was held in the Green Room.

Funeral procession in Washington

From there, the Lincoln Funeral in Washington, D.C., began on April 19 at 2:00 p.m., when the President's body left the White House for the last time, and travelled down Pennsylvania Avenue to the Capitol Rotunda. Six gray horses carried the President's coffin. Despite an enormous crowd, the procession was nearly silent, except for a dim drumming and the sounds of the horses' hooves. Once the procession reached the Capitol, the President's body was escorted up the very steps on which he was inaugurated less than two months earlier. The coffin was brought into the Capitol Rotunda, where his body remained alone overnight.

The following day, the Rotunda was opened for a public viewing of the President. At around 7:00 a.m., the public began flowing through the Capitol, with a steady stream coming through consistently until the sun began to set.

On April 21, the President's body finally left Washington, for the beginning of a long train route back to Illinois. The train embarked on a nationwide viewing, which began in nearby Baltimore, Maryland. From there, the train moved on to the following sites: Harrisburg, Pennsylvania; Philadelphia; New

York City; Albany, New York; Buffalo; Cleveland; Columbus, Indianapolis; Michigan City, Indiana; Chicago; and, finally, Springfield, Illinois. The President's body lay in state at each location.

Lincoln's funeral was, and still is, widely regarded as the greatest funeral in the history of the United States. Never before, or since, has a single person passed through so many communities: though the President's body only rested in state in the previous communities, the funeral train passed through over 400 towns and cities.

Once in Springfield, the President lay in state a final time before being brought to the Oak Ridge Cemetery for burial. Alongside his son William Wallace Lincoln's body, the two were moved to a receiving vault on May 4th, 1865. The Lincoln Tomb was still under construction, and would not be complete for some years, when Lincoln was relocated.

Being the first American President assassinated, President Lincoln's death shook the nation to its core. After four years of unprecedented trauma, Lincoln had guided the nation through the Civil War, only to become in some ways one of its last victims. On May 23-24, to commemorate the end of the war, regiments of the Union Armies held a Grand Review of the Armies, parading through the streets of Washington D.C. Famous leaders like Generals Sherman and Grant were present, as were the government's top officials, but Lincoln's absence could not help but be felt by everyone.

Still, it's necessary to remember that his untimely death transformed him into a martyr and dramatically altered his legacy in American history. At the time of his death, Lincoln's image transformed overnight. On April 14, Lincoln was a solid, but controversial, President. For much of his presidency, he was under attack from all sides: Democrats considered him a power grabber disregarding the Constitution, Republicans didn't like his policy plans for Reconstruction, many didn't respect the Westerner they considered to be too coarse, and the South despised him. Put simply, Lincoln may have been appreciated among freed blacks in the South and people in the North for leading the nation through the Civil War, but he was not the titanic figure he is today.

However, in the generation after the Civil War, Lincoln became an American deity and one of the most written about men in history. Furthermore, the gravity of his legacy skyrocketed on the morning of April 15. The tragedy and unexpectedness of his death, coupled with its violence, helped turn Lincoln into a martyr, and Lincoln's accomplishments were solidified. Lincoln had ended slavery in the South and ensured that the Union remained undivided. He had also put in place Reconstruction policies that would help lead to sectional reconciliation and the Civil War Amendments, which ended slavery, gave minorities voting rights, and provided equal protection of citizens against the actions of the states. Without question, these accomplishments earned Lincoln a place in the pantheon of American legends.

At the same time, Lincoln had clearly reached the apex of his presidency with the defeat of the Confederacy. With a second term fully ahead of him, there's no telling how mired his legacy would have been by Reconstruction, which pitted Radical Republicans against President Johnson and Democrats. The Republicans wished to subject the South to harsher treatment than Johnson's conciliatory policies, and even though many in the South were allowed to take loyalty oaths, many continued to intimidate, suppress, and kill blacks, remaining "unreconstructed". Eventually, the South was put under martial law and turned into military districts put under the control of the federal army. Reconstruction would not officially end until 1876, and while there's no question that Lincoln would have governed more competently than Andrew Johnson, there's also no question that Reconstruction during his second term would have tarnished his record, and ultimately, his legacy.

Nevertheless, those alternatives remain what ifs, and historians today widely consider Lincoln the country's greatest President. There is equally little question that his assassination helped propel him to that position. With his tragic death, the aura of martyr would not surround Lincoln, and his record might have looked far different if he left office in 1868. The legacy of Abraham Lincoln would not have been possible without the events of April 14, 1865, and the actions of one man: John Wilkes Booth.

Booth's Letter

Shortly after the assassination, a letter Booth had written in the months leading up to the assassination was published by the *New York Times*. The letter read:

"_____. _____. 1864

MY DEAR SIR, -- You may use this as you think most. But as some may wish to know when, who and why, and as I know not how to direct, I give it (in the words of your master)

'TO WHOM IT MAY CONCERN':

Right or wrong. God judge me, not man. For be my motive good or bad, of one thing I am sure, the lasting condemnation of the North.

I love peace more than life. Have loved the Union beyond expression. For four years have I waited, hoped and prayed for the dark clouds to break, and for a restoration of our former sunshine. To wait longer would be a crime. All hope for peace is dead. My prayers have proved as idle as my hopes. God's will be done. I go to see and share the bitter end.

I have ever held the South were right. The very nomination of ABRAHAM LINCOLN, four years ago, spoke plainly, war -- war upon Southern rights and institutions. His election proved it. 'Await an overt act.' Yes, till you are bound and plundered. What folly! The South was wise. Who thinks of argument or patience when the finger of his enemy presses on the trigger? In a foreign war I, too, could say, 'country, right or wrong.' But in a struggle such as ours, (where the brother tries to pierce the brother's heart,) for God's sake, choose the right. When a country like this spurns justice from her side she forfeits the allegiance of every honest freeman, and should leave him, untrameled by any fealty soever, to act as his conscience may approve.

People of the North, to hate tyranny, to love liberty and justice, to strike at wrong and oppression, was the teaching of our fathers. The study of our early history will not let me forget it, and may it never.

This country was formed for the white, not for the black man. And looking upon African Slavery from the same stand-point held by the noble framers of our constitution. I for one, have ever considered if one of the greatest blessings (both for themselves and us,) that God has ever bestowed upon a favored nation. Witness heretofore our wealth and power; witness their elevation and enlightenment above their race elsewhere. I have lived among it most of my life, and have seen less harsh treatment from master to man than I have beheld in the North from father to son. Yet, Heaven knows, no one would be willing to do more for the negro race than I, could I but see a way to still better their condition.

But LINCOLN's policy is only preparing the way for their total annihilation. The South are not, nor have they been fighting for the continuance of slavery. The first battle of Bull Run did away with that idea. Their causes since for war have been as noble and greater far than those that urged our fathers on Even should we allow they were wrong at the beginning of this contest, cruelty and injustice have made the wrong become the right, and they stand now (before the wonder and admiration of the world) as a noble band of patriotic heroes. Hereafter, reading of their deeds, Thermopylae will be forgotten.

When I aided in the capture and execution of JOHN BROWN (who was a murderer on our Western border, and who was fairly tried and convicted, before an impartial judge and jury, of treason, and who, by the way, has since been made a god), I was proud of my little share in the transaction, for I deemed it my duty, and that I was helping our common country to perform an act of justice. But what was a crime in poor JOHN BROWN is now considered (by themselves) as the greatest and only virtue of the whole Republican party. Strange transmigration! Vice to become a virtue, simply because more indulge in it.

I thought men, as now, that the Abolitionists were the only traitors in the land, and that the entire party deserved the same fate of poor old BROWN, not because they wish to abolish slavery but on account of the means they have ever endeavored to use to effect that abolition. If BROWN were living I doubt whether he himself would set slavery against the Union. Most or many in the North do, and openly curse the Union, if the South are to return and retain a single right guaranteed to them by every tie which we once revered as sacred. The South can make no choice. It is either extermination or slavery for themselves (worse than death) to draw from. I know my choice.

I have also studied hard to discover upon what grounds the right of a State to secede has been denied, when our very name, United States, and the Declaration of Independence, both provide for secession. But there is no time for words. I write in haste. I know how foolish I shall be deemed for undertaking such a step as this, where, on the one side, I have many friends, and everything to make me happy, where my profession alone has gained me an income of more than twenty thousand dollars a year, and where my great personal ambition in my profession has such a great field for labor. On the other hand, the South have never bestowed upon me one kind word; a place now where I have no friends, except beneath the sod; a place where I must either become a private soldier or a beggar. To give up all of the former for the latter, besides my mother and sisters whom I love so dearly, (although they so widely differ with me in opinion,) seems insane; but God is my judge. I love justice more than I do a country that disowns it; more than fame and wealth; more (Heaven pardon me if wrong,) more than a happy home. I have never been upon a battle-field; but O, my countrymen, could you all but see the reality or effects of this horrid war, as I have seen them, (in every State save Virginia.) I know you would think like me, and would pray the Almighty to create in the Northern mind a sense of right and justice, (even should it possess no seasoning of mercy,) and that he would dry up this sea of blood between us, which is daily growing wider. Alas! poor country, is she to meet her threatened doom? Four years ago I would have given a thousand lives to see her remain (as I had always known her) powerful and unbroken. And even now, I would hold my life as naught to see her what she was. O, my friends, if the fearful scenes of the past four years had never been enacted, or if what has been had been but a frightful dream, from which we could now awake, with what overflowing hearts could we bless our God and pray for his continued favor. How I have loved the old flag, can never now be known. A few years since and the entire world could boast of none so pure and spotless. But I have of late been seeing and hearing of the bloody deeds of which she has been made the emblem, and would shudder to think how changed she had grown. O, how I have longed to see her break from the mist of blood and death that circles round her folds, spoiling her beauty and tarnishing her honor. But no, day by day has she been dragged deeper and deeper into cruelty and oppression, till now (in my eyes) her once bright red stripes look like bloody gashes on the face of Heaven. I look now upon my early admiration of her glories as a dream. My love (as things stand to-day) is for the South alone. Nor do I deem it a dishonor in attempting to make for her a prisoner of this man, to whom she owes so much of misery. If success attends me, I go penniless to her side. They say she has found that 'last ditch' which the North have so long derided, and been endeavoring to force her in, forgetting they are our brothers, and that it's impolitic to goad an enemy to madness. Should I reach her in safety and find it true, I will proudly beg permission to triumph or die in that same 'ditch' by her side.

A Confederate doing duty upon his own responsibility. J. WILKES BOOTH."

Bibliography

Deeb, Michael J. *The Lincoln Assassination: Who Helped John Wilkes Booth Murder Lincoln?* Iuniverse.com: 2011.

Kauffman, Michael. *American Brutus.* New York: Random House. 2004.

Luthern, Ashley. "Documenting the Death of an Assassin." *Smithsonian Magazine.* May 6, 2011.
http://www.smithsonianmag.com/history-archaeology/Documenting-the-Death-of-an-Assassin.html

O'Reilly, Bill. *Killing Lincoln: The Shocking Assassination that Changed America Forever.*
    New York: Henry Holt, 2011.

Schwartz, Barry. *Abraham Lincoln and the Forge of National Memory.* Chicago: University of
    Chicago Press, 2000.

Made in the USA
Columbia, SC
04 June 2019